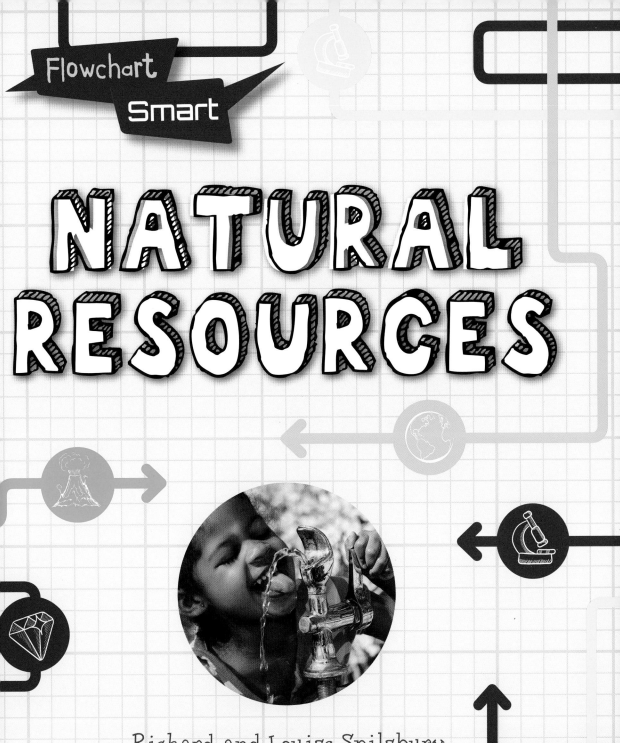

Flowchart Smart

NATURAL RESOURCES

Richard and Louise Spilsbury

Gareth Stevens
PUBLISHING

Please visit our website, **www.garethstevens.com**.
For a free color catalog of all our high-quality books,
call toll free 1-800-542-2595 or fax 1-877-542-2596.

Cataloging-in-Publication Data
Names: Spilsbury, Richard. | Spilsbury, Louise.
Title: Natural resources / Richard and Louise Spilsbury.
Description: New York : Gareth Stevens Publishing, 2019. | Series: Flowchart smart | Includes glossary
and index.
Identifiers: ISBN 9781538234884 (pbk.) | ISBN 9781538234891 (library bound)
Subjects: LCSH: Natural resources--Juvenile literature.
Classification: LCC HC85.S677 2019 | DDC 333.7--dc23

First Edition

Published in 2019 by
Gareth Stevens Publishing
111 East 14th Street, Suite 349
New York, NY 10003

Produced for Gareth Stevens by Calcium
Editors: Sarah Eason and Harriet McGregor
Designer: Emma DeBanks
Picture researcher: Rachel Blount

Picture credits: Cover: Shutterstock: Denk Creative; Inside: Shutterstock: Alinabel: p. 23; Eganova
Antonina: p. 5c; Bannafarsai_Stock: p. 29t; Chromatos: p. 17; Curraheeshutter: p. 35t; Denk Creative:
pp. 4t, 4bl, 13, 25r; Designua: p. 43; ES_SO: pp. 40–41; FabrikaSimf: p. 31; Fairy-N: p. 28r; Geo-grafika:
p. 33t; D. Hammonds: p. 1; Jerry Horbert: p. 20; Images72: p. 15t; Irin-k: p. 18; Ammit Jack: p. 24b;
Amy Johansson: pp. 20–21; Anan Kaewkhammul: pp. 24–25; Kamieshkova: p. 26t; Zivica Kerkez: p. 5t;
Kucherov Pro: pp. 28–29; Thomas La Mela: pp. 44–45; Lapas77: p. 27; Puripat Lertpunyaroj: p. 41t;
Lmfoto: p. 26; Macknimal: pp. 10–11; Marcovarro: pp. 14–15; Maridav: pp. 4–5; Riccardo Mayer: p. 13t;
Nadiia 80: p. 9; Phuong D. Nguyen: pp. 12–13; Nikiteev Konstantin: p. 7br; NoPainNoGain: pp. 34–35;
Oleandra: pp. 36–37; Patrick Poendl: p. 39t; Alexander Raths: p. 19; Rawpixel.com: p. 45b; Smileus: pp.
6–7; Studio23: pp. 38–39; Vovan: p. 7t; Sergiy Zavgorodny: p. 11t; Rudmer Zwerver: pp. 32–33.

Printed in the United States of America

CPSIA compliance information: Batch #CW19GS: For further information contact Gareth Stevens, New York, New York at 1-800-542-2595.

Contents

Chapter 1
Gifts from Nature

Natural resources are the materials and substances that we take from the **environment**, such as water, soil, and rocks. These resources are a natural part of the land, oceans, and **atmosphere** and they are necessary or useful to humans.

Some resources are so important to us that we could not survive without them. These vital resources include the air that we breathe, the water that we drink, and the food that we eat. There is also a wide range of natural resources that we use to make our lives better or easier. These resources include fuels such as coal, which we burn for warmth, and metals to make cars and computers.

Natural resources are not made by people; they come from nature. The plants, water, air, and rocks in this picture are natural resources.

Some natural resources are used virtually as we find them, such as the wood used to build homes. Other resources are used to produce something new, by altering a raw material. For example, we use crude oil drilled from underground to make plastic. This plastic is used to create items such as tennis rackets and kayaks. You would never guess that they started life as a sticky, black liquid.

These items were made from natural resources. The table is made from wood, the laptop contains metal mined from the ground, and the coffee is ground from coffee beans.

Get Smart!

People living in rich countries consume up to 10 times more natural resources per person than those in the poorest countries.

The Sun

One of our most important natural resources is not even on planet Earth. The heat and light **energy** that reaches us from the sun makes life on Earth possible and provides us with many of our most vital resources.

The sun is 93 million miles (150 million km) from Earth. Without its heat and light, our planet would be nothing but an empty ball of ice-covered rock. Like other stars in the universe, the sun is a sphere of burning hot **gases**. We use its light to see by, and its heat generates our weather and powers the **water cycle**. It keeps some of the world's water in a liquid state that we can use and powers virtually all **life processes** on Earth.

The sun provides green plants with energy that they use to make their own food and grow. The plants provide us with food. To make their own food, plants use water and a gas called carbon dioxide. They absorb, or soak up, water from the soil through roots, and take in carbon dioxide from the air through tiny holes called stomata in their leaves. Plants combine these two ingredients to make food in the form of glucose, or sugar. To do this they need energy. They trap the energy in sunlight using a green pigment in their leaves called chlorophyll. This whole process is called **photosynthesis**.

Get Smart!

The sun is one of 100 billion stars in the galaxy. It is special because it is close enough to Earth to allow life to survive here.

In spring, new green leaves grow, ready to absorb sunlight and grow through the spring and summer period.

Without sunlight, these huge fields of corn would not grow and there would be no corn on the cob to eat.

Get flowchart smart!

How Photosynthesis Works

Follow the steps in this flowchart to learn how plants use sunlight to grow.

Plants absorb water from the soil through their roots.

Plants use the glucose to live and grow.

The food they make is in the form of glucose.

Flowchart Smart

sun

They take in carbon dioxide from the air through tiny holes in their leaves called stomata.

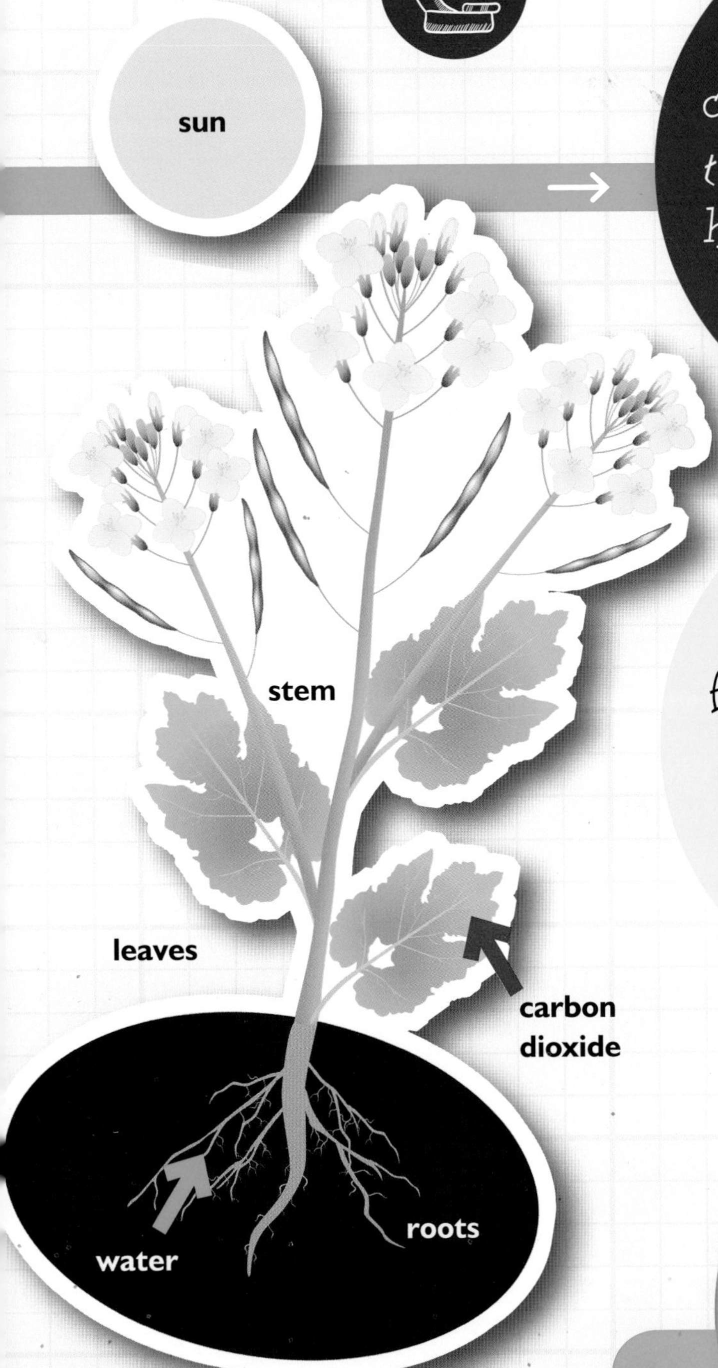

stem

Plants trap energy from sunlight using a green pigment in their leaves called chlorophyll.

leaves

carbon dioxide

roots

water

They use this energy to combine water and carbon dioxide to make food.

9

Chapter 2
Vital Resources

Vital resources are those upon which our lives depend. Water, soil, and air are all vital resources. Air is one of the most important resources of all. We cannot see, smell, or taste air, but the gases it contains are essential for life on Earth.

Air contains a mixture of gases: 78 percent nitrogen, 21 percent oxygen, and smaller amounts of other gases, such as **water vapor** and carbon dioxide. Humans need oxygen to live. We breathe in air to get oxygen. Oxygen is carried in our blood to **cells** all around the body. Chemical reactions take place between oxygen and sugars from food. These reactions release energy that we use to move, grow, and make new parts, such as new skin cells, when we are injured. This energy production process is called **respiration**.

Combustion, or burning, is a chemical process in which a substance reacts rapidly with oxygen and produces heat and light. Combustion requires three essential ingredients: oxygen, fuel, and a spark or heat to start the process. Without oxygen, a fuel will not burn. Rocket engines, jet engines, and vehicle combustion engines all depend on burning fuel in oxygen to produce power. Oxygen also keeps natural gas burning in power plants to make electricity.

Forest fires burn rapidly in windy weather. Wind increases the supply of oxygen to the fire.

When people swim deep underwater they must take a tank of air with them in order to breathe.

Get Smart!

Earth is the only known planet on which fire can burn, because it is the only one that has enough oxygen for combustion to take place.

Water

Humans can survive for weeks without food, but only a few days without water. Humans need freshwater, not the salt water found in the world's oceans. Less than 0.025 percent of all the water on Earth is usable freshwater.

As well as using water to drink, we use water in our homes and daily lives for cooking, washing, cleaning, and to remove waste. We use water to wash automobiles, water lawns, and fill swimming pools. In cities, water fills fountains and is used to clean streets. Much of the water we use is piped to our homes across long distances. It comes from rivers, lakes, and artificial lakes called **reservoirs**, or from sources of water called aquifers that collect deep underground.

Farming is the most water-dependent industry. On average, agriculture uses 69 percent of the world's available freshwater, mostly for watering fields of crops. Other industries, such as power plants that make electricity and factories that produce metals, wood, paper, plastic products, chemicals, and gasoline, use 19 percent of the world's available freshwater. The water is used as a raw material, for example in making processed foods, and is also used to process, wash, cool, or transport a product.

These people are washing colorful clothes in the water of the River Yamuna in Agra, India.

People should drink about eight glasses of water a day and even more when it is hot.

Get Smart!

The average family home in the United States uses more than 300 gallons (1,364 l) of water every day. Up to three-quarters of this water is used indoors.

Soil

Soil is one of the world's most important natural resources. Together with air and water it is the basis for life on planet Earth. Farmers need **fertile** soil to grow plants for us to eat, and we need food to survive.

Soil is a mixture of tiny pieces of rock, water, air, and **organic** matter. Organic matter comes from decayed plants and animals: either from the waste they produce when they are alive, or from their bodies after they die. Topsoil is the surface layer of soil in which plants grow. Healthy, fertile topsoil is rich in organic matter and the other ingredients plants need to grow such as water, oxygen, and **minerals** from rock. Topsoil can take millions of years to form.

Plants also replenish air, another of the world's most important natural resources. Plants take in water and carbon dioxide for photosynthesis. Water is made up of two different kinds of atoms: oxygen and hydrogen. During photosynthesis, the two types of atoms are separated. Hydrogen combines with carbon dioxide to make glucose and oxygen leaves the plant through the stomata on the leaves. This supply of oxygen builds up in our atmosphere and is a vital part of the air that we breathe.

Get Smart!

Soil is alive! **Bacteria** and other tiny living things make their homes in soil. They help break down the organic matter in soil and keep it healthy and fertile.

Apples grow well in fertile, sandy soil. The more fertile the soil, the better the apple harvest.

Worms help break down organic matter and increase the amount of air and water that gets into the soil.

Get flowchart smart!

How Plants Make Oxygen

The steps in this flowchart explain how plants produce and release oxygen.

Plants take in water and carbon dioxide during photosynthesis.

The plant releases most of the oxygen into the air through the stomata on the leaves.

This supply of oxygen is a vital part of the air that we breathe.

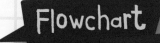
Flowchart Smart

16

Water is made of two different kinds of atom: oxygen and hydrogen. During photosynthesis, the oxygen and hydrogen atoms separate.

The hydrogen combines with carbon dioxide to make glucose.

oxygen atom

hydrogen atom

water

Chapter 3
Plant and Animal Resources

Plant resources are the source of food for almost every living thing on Earth. Plants and animals are also used to make a wide variety of other useful products.

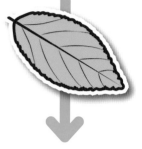

Plants are known as producers because they produce their own food through photosynthesis. Animals cannot make their own food, so they have to eat. They are consumers. Many animals, such as rabbits and cows, eat plants and use energy stored in the plants to live and grow. Other animals eat plant-eating animals. For example, foxes eat rabbits to get the energy they need to survive. In this way energy from the sun, originally trapped by plants, is transferred from one living thing to the next. This is called a food chain.

Grass uses the sun's energy to grow. Cows eat the grass. People drink cows' milk and eat beef. In this way, the sun's energy passes up the food chain.

Plants and animals provide us with many different kinds of food, from fruit juice and coffee, to cereals, salads, and hamburgers. Plant parts, such as cinnamon bark and ginger root, are used to make spices that add flavor to our food. We catch and eat fish and shellfish from the oceans, and use seaweed as an ingredient in products such as toothpaste, cosmetics, and paints. Many of the medicines we use are made or derived from plant parts, and essential oils are extracted from plant parts to make perfumes.

Many different natural resources—including the sun, plants, coal or gas, and air—are involved in creating your summer barbecue.

Get Smart!

About 70 percent of the world's plant species that are known to be useful in cancer treatments are only found in rainforests. There are many rainforest plants still to be documented by science. Scientists expect that many more of them will be useful for medicines.

Wood and Textiles

Plant parts are used to clothe and house people. Garments and buildings not only keep us comfortable, they also provide us with pleasure.

Wood is the hard inner part of a tree's trunk and branches. When trees are cut down and the wood dries out it can then be cut and carved to make walls, window frames, decks, and furniture. Wood from trees is also used to make objects such as baseball bats, guitars, and boats. Wood is cut into small pieces and crushed to make wood pulp. Wood pulp is used to make paper for newspapers, books and magazines, and packaging.

Some of the materials we use to make clothing come from animals. Leather is animal skin that has been treated in order to preserve it. It is used to make shoes and jackets. Wool is made from the hair that forms the coat of a sheep, goat, or similar animal. Other fabrics come from plants. Cotton is made from the **fibers** that grow around the seed of the cotton plant, and linen is made from the fibers of the flax plant. One way to make textiles from the tough stems of bamboo is to crush the plants into a mush, comb out the fibers, and spin them into yarn, which can then be woven into fabric.

The entire cotton plant is used. The fibers are made into fabrics, the seed into animal feed, and the stalks are added back into the soil in the cotton field.

Trees are a natural resource that can be renewed by planting trees to replace those that were cut down.

Get flowchart smart!

How Food Chains Work

See how food chains work by following the steps in this flowchart.

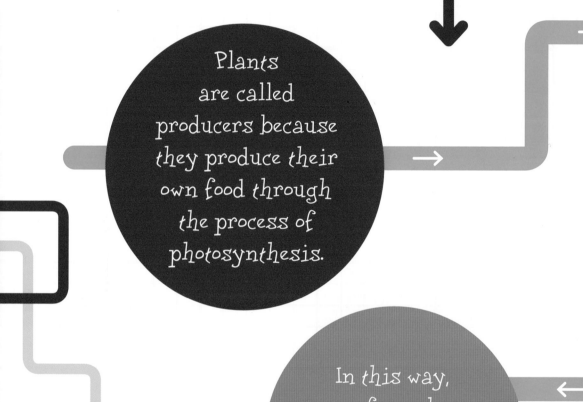

Plants are called producers because they produce their own food through the process of photosynthesis.

In this way, energy from the sun is transferred between living things in a food chain.

Flowchart
Smart

Animals are called consumers because they cannot make their own food. Some animals eat plants and use energy stored in *the* plant's body to live and grow.

Other animals eat plant-eating animals to get the energy they need *to* survive.

sun

plant

grasshopper

songbird

snake

owl

Chapter 4
Raw Materials

Earth's crust contains many minerals and other materials that are very useful to us. Minerals are nonliving substances found in rocks. To extract these useful natural resources, people must dig them out of the ground. These raw materials are made into a wide range of different things, from parking lots to plastic canoes.

Plastic is a material made from crude oil and natural gas, both of which are extracted from deep underground. There are more than 10,000 different kinds of plastics. Most plastics can be made into any shape or color. They are strong, long-lasting, and lightweight. They can be rigid, such as in a plastic canoe, flexible like a plastic rope, opaque like a plastic door, or transparent like a plastic bottle. Plastic can even be made to look like other materials such as leather, wood, or silk.

Kayaks made from plastics are strong, waterproof, and can be very colorful, too.

Over one-fourth of the crude oil produced in the United States is extracted from under the sea in the Gulf of Mexico.

Crude oil was formed underground more than 300 million years ago.

When crude oil and natural gas have been extracted from the ground, they are transported to a refinery in large ships or trucks called tankers, or through long pipes. A refinery is a factory that changes the oil and gas into other materials, such as useful chemicals called polymers. Polymers are transported to a plastics factory where they are converted into plastic in the form of small pellets. Plastic pellets are taken to other factories where they are melted down. The **molten** plastic is then poured into molds. When it sets hard it forms different products.

Crystals and Metals

Crystals are solid materials that form in regular repeating shapes. Most metals are composed of crystals. Different kinds of crystals and metals have different properties, which make these natural resources useful for different products.

Some of the minerals that form under high **pressures** or temperatures deep within Earth's interior are crystals. The most valuable are rare and colorful gems, such as rubies and sapphires, which can be cut and polished to make jewelry. As well as being prized for their beauty, diamond crystals are so hard that they are used to make cutting tools. Diamond-tipped discs are used to cut bricks and concrete. People also make crystals from raw materials. Silicon minerals are made into crystals used in computer chips.

Crystals come in different colors. Rubies, like this one, are red.

Gold is a fairly soft metal, so it can be beaten into thin sheets or made into shapes.

Get Smart!

Tiny quartz crystals are used in quartz watches. The crystals vibrate a certain number of times per second when electricity is passed through them, making them useful for keeping time.

Metals such as iron, aluminum, and copper are found as metallic minerals inside rocks called ores. Gold metal has a warm color and sheen and is quite rare, so it is used to make precious jewelry. Heat and electricity pass through copper quickly and easily, so copper is used to make heating pipes and electric wires. Aluminum is lightweight, soft, and flexible. It is used to make products such as soda cans, aircraft, and automobile bodies.

Construction Materials

Mineral resources are used to construct most of the homes, offices, factories, airports, and other buildings around the world.

Some older, historic buildings were made from large pieces of solid stone or had walls lined with pieces of beautiful and expensive solid stone such as marble. Most buildings today are made from bricks or smaller pieces of stone. Bricks are formed from clay, which is baked in molds until it sets hard. Bricks and stones are held together with cement, which is a powdery substance made from lime and clay, mixed with water. When sand, gravel, and water are added to the mix, this makes concrete, which is used for walls, driveways, and parking lots.

Strong, solid materials are ideal for constructing buildings, but we also need materials that allow light to pass through them. Glass windows are used for this purpose. Glass is made by melting sand, which contains the mineral silicon, with crushed limestone rock and soda ash in a hot oven. The melted mixture is rolled flat while it is still liquid, before it sets into hard glass. Glass is also used to make lenses and mirrors, and thin strands of glass are used to make fiber-optic cables that transmit digital data over long distances in the form of light signals.

In many countries, the construction industry is the largest user of natural resources.

When wet, concrete can be poured to fit a shape or create a level floor. Then it sets hard.

Get Smart!

Gypsum is a soft rock that is used to make wallboard, some cements, and plaster. Gypsum forms deep underground from the remains of shellfish buried beneath the ocean floor. Over millions of years the remains are squashed into rock.

Get flowchart smart!

Making Plastic Products

Follow this flowchart to find out how plastic products are made.

Crude oil and natural gas are extracted from the ground. They are transported to a refinery.

When it sets hard it forms different plastic products.

The molten plastic is poured into molds.

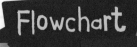
Flowchart Smart

In the refinery, oil and gas are changed into other materials, such as chemicals called polymers.

Polymers are transported to a plastics factory where they are converted into small plastic pellets.

Plastic pellets are taken to other factories where they are melted down.

Chapter 5
Fossil Fuels

Oil, coal, and natural gas are fossil fuels. They formed gradually over millions of years from the remains of dead plants and animals. Fossil fuels provide energy to power a wide variety of machines and to create electricity.

Fuels are materials that we burn to release energy in the form of light, heat, or movement. The majority of oil pumped up from underground is used to make gasoline and diesel, which are liquid fuels. They are used to power cars, trucks, planes, and ships. Natural gas is used for cooking, heating buildings, and heating water. Coal is used in steel and cement factories.

These heaps of coal are ready to be burned in a coal-fired power plant. Smoke is released through the narrow chimneys into the atmosphere.

Electricity powers millions of different machines, including lights, computers, and televisions. In countries such as the United States, fossil fuels provide about two-thirds of the electricity. In a coal-fired power plant, coal is burned to boil water and make steam. The steam pushes against the angled blades of a **turbine**, which is a bit like a propeller. The motion of the turbine spins coils of wire inside the **generator**. Inside the coils of wire is a magnet. The motion generates an electric current in the wires.

Coal is a combustible black rock that runs in veins through the rock beneath Earth's surface.

Get Smart!

Globally, around 80 percent of the world's electricity is generated by burning fossil fuels.

How Fossil Fuels Form

Coal formed from dead plant material, mostly from forests of giant ferns, reeds, and mosses that grew in swamps around 300 million years ago. Oil and gas mostly formed from dead ocean animals.

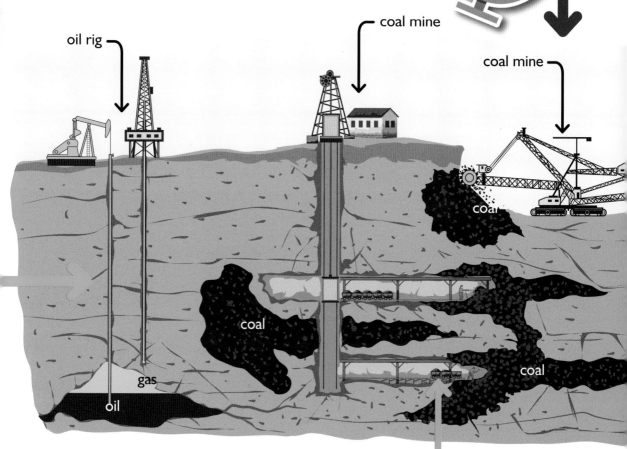

oil rig

coal mine

coal mine

coal

coal

gas

oil

coal

After the plants in ancient forests died, their remains collected in layers in the damp swamp. Here, the remains rotted incredibly slowly. Over time, more layers of dirt and water washed over the lower layers of remains, one on top of the other. The weight of the top layers pressed down on the lower layers. Heat and pressure produced chemical and physical changes in the plant remains. In time, the remains of the plants became coal.

This image shows how different fossil fuels are buried deep underground.

Fossil fuels can trace the source of their energy back to the sun. When the plants were alive they trapped the sun's energy. This energy passed along the food chain. The energy stored in the plants and animal bodies became part of the fossil fuels. It is this energy that is released when the fuels are burned.

oil rig

Earth's crust

gas

oil

Sometimes, oil and gas platforms burn natural gas that cannot be captured and stored easily.

Oil and gas formed in a similar way to coal, through high pressures and hot temperatures underground. The difference is that oil and gas formed from the remains of microscopic sea animals that became buried in sand and mud at the bottom of ancient oceans. Their remains gradually turned into drops of oil and bubbles of gas that collected in spaces between layers of rock. Oil is taken from the ground at an oil rig, and coal is mined.

Get flowchart smart!

How Coal Formed

Follow the steps in this flowchart to discover how coal formed.

After the plants in ancient forests died, their remains collected in layers in the damp swamp where they grew.

In time, the remains of the plants became coal.

Flowchart
Smart

The remains rotted very, very slowly.

Over time, more layers of dirt and water washed over the remains, one on top of the other.

The weight of the top layers pressed down on the lower layers. Heat and pressure produced chemical and physical changes in the plant remains.

Chapter 6
Renewable Energy

Fossil fuels are a form of **nonrenewable** energy because once they are used up, it will take millions of years to form more. Increasingly, countries around the world are using **renewable** forms of energy instead, such as wind, moving water, and sunlight. Renewable energy will never run out.

There is a lot of energy in strong winds. Giant wind turbines capture this energy. Wind turbines are tall towers with rotating blades. When wind hits the angled, flat surfaces of the blades, it makes the turbine rotate. This movement energy is used to turn a generator, which produces electricity. In order to produce a large amount of energy, great numbers of wind turbines are built on windy spots. These are called wind farms.

Hydropower is the power of moving water. Most hydroelectric power plants are built across rivers. A barrier called a **dam** stops or slows the flow of water and creates a reservoir behind it. Some of this water is released through pipes that drop down from the reservoir. As gravity pulls the water down, it flows over a turbine, making the turbine blades rotate. The turbine drives a generator that makes electricity. Some hydroelectric power plants are built at sea. They use wave or **tidal** power to generate electricity.

The turbines in the Mooserboden Dam, in Austria, are behind the dam walls.

Wind turbine blades can be 200 feet (60 m) long. The towers can be as tall as a 20-story building.

Get Smart!

Experts believe that if the increase in wind farms continues at current rates, one-third of the world's electricity will be provided by wind power by 2050.

Power from Heat

Electricity can be generated from the sun, or even from Earth's own heat. Solar power plants use energy from the sun, while geothermal power plants tap into the heat energy deep beneath Earth's surface.

Solar panel electricity systems are also known as photovoltaics (PV). The PV cells capture the sun's energy. When light shines on the cell it creates an electric field across the layers. The stronger the sunshine, the more electricity is produced. Groups of cells are mounted together in panels that can either be attached to a roof or wall, or on supports on the ground. The electricity produced can be used to run machines in homes and offices.

Temperatures deep within our planet are so high that they can melt rock. Heat energy created and stored within Earth is known as geothermal energy. To use this heat to make electricity, holes are drilled down 1 mile (1.6 km) or deeper into Earth's crust. The wells collect pockets of steam and very hot water. The steam and hot water are brought to the surface where they rotate turbines. The turbines drive generators that produce electricity.

The cells in photovoltaic solar panels do not need direct sunlight to work. They can still generate some electricity on a cloudy day.

This swimming pool in Iceland contains geothermally heated water.

Get Smart!

Sometimes, hot rocks containing reservoirs of steam and hot water are found near Earth's surface. In these places, the steam and hot water are carried through pipes and are used to heat homes and buildings directly.

Get flowchart smart!

Geothermal Power Stations in Action

The steps in this flowchart explain how geothermal power stations work.

Holes are drilled down to at least 1 mile (1.6 km) beneath Earth's surface.

The steam and hot water are used to rotate turbines.

The turbines drive generators that produce electricity.

Flowchart Smart

These wells collect pockets of steam and hot water created by Earth's internal heat.

The steam and hot water are brought to the surface.

steam

generator makes electricity

heat

Protecting Natural Resources

A major advantage of renewable energy is that it does not release gases that **pollute** the atmosphere. Burning fossil fuels releases waste gases that trap heat in Earth's atmosphere. This is causing the **greenhouse effect**, **global warming**, and climate change. Using renewable resources is one way to protect Earth from climate change.

As Earth's population grows, we take more and more resources from nature. We use more freshwater, cut down more trees, deplete fish stocks in the ocean, and destroy fertile land by overfarming it. We can reduce overuse by buying and using less in the first place, and **recycling** and reusing more of the products we do have.

Protecting natural resources is vital for the health of the planet. All natural resources are connected in some way. If one is damaged or destroyed, it affects the supply or quality of others. For example, if freshwater is used up in one area, the soil, plant and animal life, and even the air in that area will be damaged. Humans need to protect Earth's natural resources to ensure we have enough for the future and can continue to thrive on Earth.

The world population is expected to reach 8.5 billion by 2030. We need to reuse and recycle everything we can so that our planet can support all of those people.

Our use of natural resources is **unsustainable**. Today, humans use the equivalent of 1.6 Earths to provide the resources we use and absorb our waste. This means it now takes Earth one year and six months to regenerate what we use in one year.

Recycling waste is one way we can use trash as a resource.

Glossary

atmosphere The blanket of gases that surrounds Earth.

bacteria Tiny living things that can cause disease.

cells Very small parts that together form all living things.

dam A barrier built across a river.

energy The capacity to do work.

environment The natural world.

fertile Capable of producing many crops.

fibers Thread-like parts.

gases Substances that are usually colorless and invisible, take up space, and have weight, but have no shape or size of their own.

generator A machine that converts movement energy into electrical energy.

global warming An increase in temperatures around the world, caused by the greenhouse effect.

greenhouse effect The trapping of the sun's warmth by the atmosphere.

life processes The things that every living thing does: move, reproduce, sense the world around them, feed, produce, respire, and grow.

minerals The solid substances found naturally on Earth that make up rocks.

molten Melted.

nonrenewable Describes a natural resource that exists in limited supply and cannot be replaced if it is used up.

organic To do with living things or things that were once alive.

photosynthesis The process by which plants produce their own food using carbon dioxide, water, and sunlight.

pollute To add dirty or harmful substances to the air, land, or water.

pressures Pushing forces.

recycling Converting waste into something new.

renewable Describes a natural resource that can be replaced by natural processes.

reservoirs Lakes built by people to store water.

respiration A process by which living things release energy from their food.

tidal To do with the tides moving back and forth.

turbine A machine that spins when water, air, or steam moves across it.

unsustainable Not capable of continuing at the same rate or level.

water cycle The way in which water circulates between Earth's oceans, atmosphere, and land.

water vapor The gas form of water.

For More Information

Books

Grady, Colin. *Fossil Fuels*. New York, NY: Enslow Publishing, 2018.

Howell, Izzi. *Earth's Resources Geo Facts*. New York, NY: Crabtree Publishing Company, 2018.

Kopp, Megan. *Energy from Wind: Wind Farming*. New York, NY: Crabtree Publishing Company, 2016.

Sanchez, Micah. *Natural Resource Depletion*. New York, NY: PowerKids Press, 2018.

Websites

Visit NASA's Climate Kids website to find out more about climate change:
climatekids.nasa.gov/climate-change-meaning

Discover the basics about natural resources at:
www.eschooltoday.com/natural-resources/what-is-a-natural-resource.html

Click through the images to learn how people are conserving natural resources throughout the world at:
www.nationalgeographic.org/encyclopedia/conservation

Watch a slideshow about natural resources at:
studyjams.scholastic.com/studyjams/jams/science/energy-light-sound/natural-resources.htm

Index